WHY DON'T HAIRCUTS HURT?

QUESTIONS AND ANSWERS ABOUT YOUR BODY

BY **MELVIN AND GILDA BERGER**

ILLUSTRATED BY **KAREN BARNES**

SCHOLASTIC REFERENCE

Contents

KEY TO ABBREVIATIONS

cm = centimeter / centimetre
cm^2 = square centimeter / centimetre
kg = kilogram
km = kilometer / kilometre
l = liter
m^2 = square meter / metre
t = tonne

Library of Congress Cataloging-in-Publication Data

Berger, Melvin.
  Why don't haircuts hurt? / Melvin & Gilda Berger.
    p.   cm.
  Summary: Provides answers to a variety of questions about the human body, including "Why do you blush?" "Why do you need two ears?" "How strong is hair?" and "What are goose bumps?"

  1. Body, Human—Juvenile literature. 2. Human physiology—Juvenile literature. [1. Body, Human—Miscellanea. 2. Questions and answers.] I. Berger, Gilda. II. Title.
QP37.B475 1998   612—dc21   97-45874   CIP   AC
ISBN 0-590-13086-2

Book design by David Saylor and Nancy Sabato

10 9 8 7 6 5 4 3 2 1   8 9/9 0/0 01 02 03

Printed in the U.S.A.   08
First printing, November 1998

Expert readers: Dr. Ann-Judith Silverman, Department of Anatomy and Cell Biology, Columbia University, New York, NY; Dr. Adele Brodkin, Consultant in Child Psychology, Scholastic Inc., New York, NY; Jon Laking, M.A., P.T., MS.T., Annapolis, MD

FOR JACOB, A UNIQUE AND EXTRAORDINARY HUMAN BEING.
— M. AND G. BERGER

FOR MOM, MY BIGGEST FAN.
— K. BARNES

Introduction

Why read a question-and-answer book?

Because you're a kid! And kids are curious. It's natural—and important—to ask *questions* and look for *answers*. This book answers many questions that you may have:

- How much food do you eat each year?
- Why do you blush?
- What is a "charley horse"?
- What are hiccups?
- What makes blood red?
- What are goose bumps?

Many of the answers will surprise and amaze you. We hope they'll tickle your imagination. Maybe they'll lead to *more questions* calling for *more answers*. That's what being curious is all about.

Melvin Berger

Gilda Berger

YOUR HAIR AND SKIN

Why don't haircuts hurt?

Because hair is mostly keratin, a substance found in dead skin cells. And cutting dead cells doesn't hurt.

Only one part of your hair is alive. It is the part you can't see. The live part grows in hair follicles under your scalp. As live hair pushes up above the scalp, it dies. That's why haircuts don't hurt. The scissors are only cutting threads of dead skin cells!

The longest hair on record belonged to Mata Jagdamba of India. Her hair measured 13 feet, 10½ inches (417 cm). What a lot of dead cells!

What are cells?

The tiny basic units of life. Cells make up every part of your body. There are skin cells, muscle cells, bone cells, blood cells, and many other kinds of cells. Altogether, your body is made up of about 10 million million cells!

Each cell has a different shape. And each type has a special job to do. For example, the live cells in hair are rectangles. They produce the keratin that makes your hair strong.

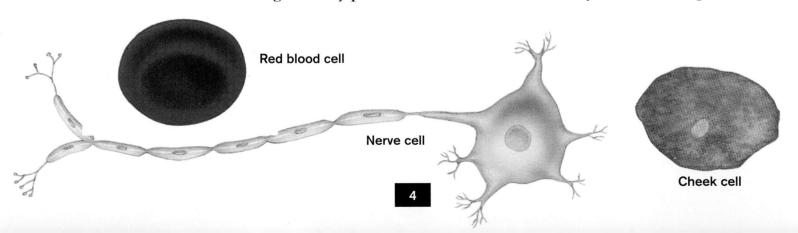

Red blood cell

Nerve cell

Cheek cell

How strong is hair?

Stronger than you'd believe. One hair can hold a 3-ounce (84 g) weight. Weave 1,000 hairs together and they can lift you and three friends. An even heavier rope of 10,000 hairs can pick up an automobile!

How many hairs do you have?

About 100,000 on your head alone! Every year you grow about 7 miles (11.2 km) of new hair. Over your lifetime you will produce nearly 600 miles (960 km) of hair—enough to reach from New York City to Detroit.

Most of the rest of your body is covered with short, tiny hairs. There are about 60 in every square inch (6.5 cm²) of skin. Some hairs are so small, they are very hard to see—but they are there. Only the palms of your hands and the soles of your feet have no hair at all!

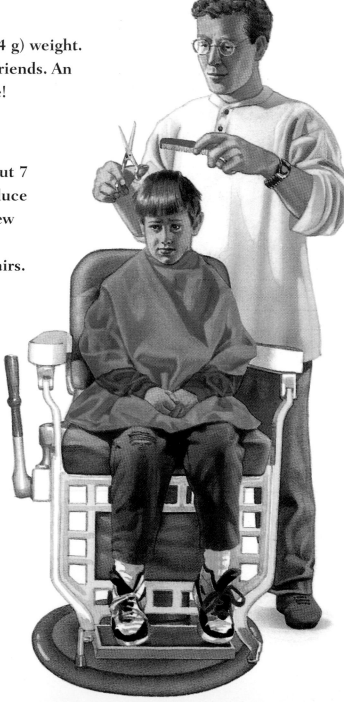

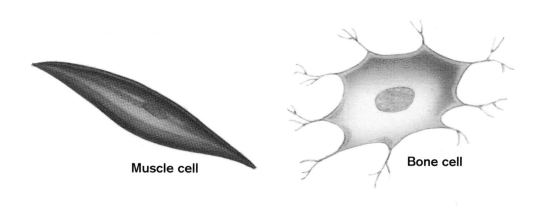

Muscle cell

Bone cell

What makes hair curly or straight?

The shape of the strand of hair. Suppose you cut a hair and look at one end under a microscope. If it is round, the hair is straight. An oval shape means wavy hair. A flattened oval tells you the hair is curly.

What gives hair its color?

All hair gets its color from melanin. Pure melanin makes hair brown or black. About 80 percent of the people in the United States have brown or black hair. If melanin contains iron or sulfur, the hair is blonde or red.

How fast does hair grow on your head?

Nearly 5 inches (12.7 cm) a year. Hair grows faster in children than in adults. It also grows faster in the morning than at night. And it grows faster in the summer than in the winter.

Diet and health also affect the growth of your hair. But don't think haircuts and shaves make hair grow faster. They don't make any difference at all.

Straight hair   **Wavy hair**   **Curly hair**

How is skin color like hair color?

Both have melanin. Skin can be any shade, from very light to very dark. It all depends on the amount of melanin produced in the skin. The skin of light-skinned people produces less melanin than that of dark-skinned people.

Why do some people tan, and others burn?

It's the melanin again! In bright sun, skin cells produce more melanin, which makes light skin tan.

Sometimes the skin is exposed to strong sunlight, and the sun's rays are so strong that they make the blood vessels swell. The skin becomes red and sore. This is sunburn. As you age, sunburn can cause wrinkles and health problems.

What are freckles?

Clumps of melanin in your skin. The small brownish spots show up mostly on the face and hands. Spending lots of time in the sun may increase the number of freckles and darken them.

Sometimes older people develop "freckles" on the backs of their hands. The dark spots show up because aging skin often produces extra amounts of melanin in certain places.

What makes your lips red?

Blood. The skin of your lips is very thin. This lets blood flowing in the tiny vessels under the skin show through.

Cross Section of the Skin

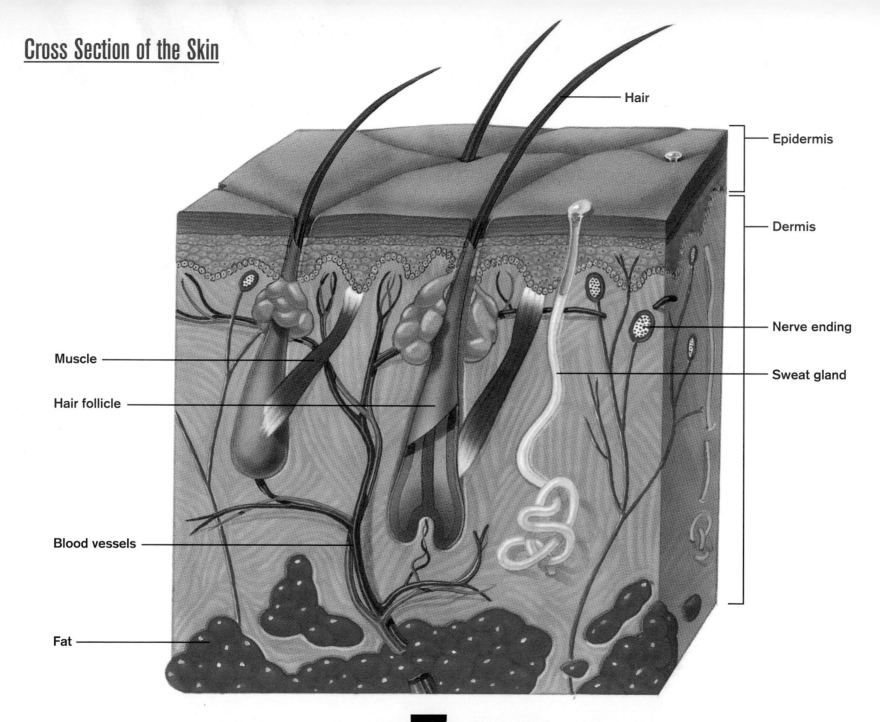

Hair

Epidermis

Dermis

Nerve ending

Muscle

Sweat gland

Hair follicle

Blood vessels

Fat

How big is the skin?

About 20 square feet (1.8 m²) in an adult. If you could lay it out flat, the skin would be big enough to cover your whole bed.

The skin has two layers. The top layer, or epidermis, is a waterproof shield between the outside world and the body tissues inside. The top layers of the epidermis are dead cells. The epidermis is about as thick as a sheet of paper.

The inner layer, or dermis, contains blood vessels and sweat glands. It is from 15 to 40 times thicker than the epidermis. Nerve endings in the dermis send messages to the brain.

The skin is thinnest on your eyelids and lips. It is thickest on the soles of your feet and the palms of your hands.

Do you keep the same skin for life?

Far from it: 50,000 tiny bits of dead skin cells fall off every *minute*! They make up about 75 percent of the dust floating around in your house. By the time you reach age 70, you'll have shed 40 pounds (18 kg) of dead skin.

Every hour your epidermis is making about one and a half million new cells to replace the lost skin cells. Just think of that. Every two weeks you get a completely new skin!

Why do you get wrinkles after a bath?

Water gets under your skin. Even though your skin is waterproof, some water does seep through. The water makes the skin underneath soggy. The wet part of the skin buckles— some parts go up, some go down. And that makes the wrinkles. But don't worry. The wrinkles don't last long—they soon go away.

Why do you have fingernails?

To protect your fingertips. Fingernails help you do many things—from peeling an orange to pressing the keys on a computer.

Fingernails are like hair. They are layers of hardened dead skin with keratin. The only part of your fingernails that is alive is the part you can't see. It takes the body about 150 days to push out a full-length fingernail. If never cut, your fingernails would grow to be nearly 12 feet (360 cm) long!

What are goose bumps?

Small bumps that appear on your skin when you're cold or frightened. The bumps occur because muscles in your skin tighten to make your hairs stand up.

Long ago, people were much hairier than today. When cold or scared, their hairs stood on end. This trapped air and made a kind of warming blanket. It also made them look larger to an enemy.

Now humans have much less hair. But they still react in the same old way to cold or fright. The skin bulges up and forms goose bumps.

How does your body cool off?

Mostly by sweating. Nerves in your skin tell your brain that you're getting hot. The brain signals the sweat glands to go to work. There are about 650 sweat glands in each square inch (6.5 cm²) of skin, or more than 2 million in all.

The glands squeeze drops of sweat out through tiny openings, or pores. There are about 2,000 pores per square inch (6.5 cm²) of skin! As the sweat dries up, your skin cools off. Your body temperature drops. On a hot day your body can lose as much as three gallons (11.4 l) of sweat! That's why it's important to drink lots of water when the temperature goes way up.

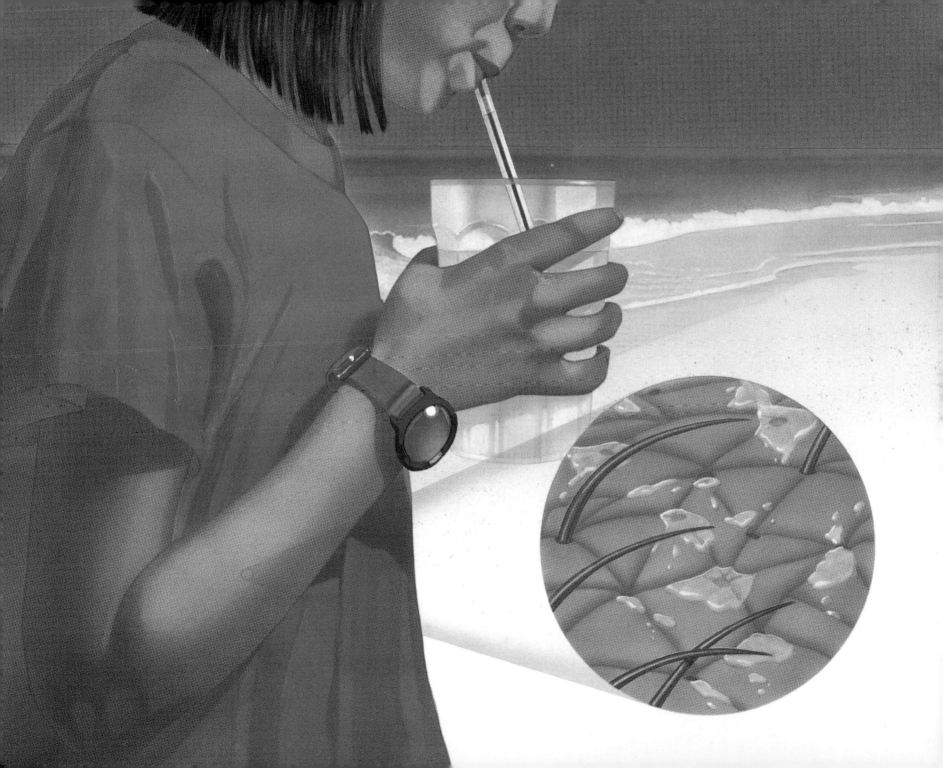

YOUR BODYWORKS

How many bones do adults have?

Each adult has 206. The bones hold up the body and protect the organs. The insides of big bones are full of a fatty substance called marrow. The marrow produces blood cells. Bones also have blood vessels and nerves.

More than half of all bones in the body are found in the hands, wrists, feet, and ankles. Many of them are very small. Adults have 27 bones in the hand alone.

Do you get more bones as you grow older?

No. In fact, babies have more bones than grown-ups do! At birth, you have about 300 bones. As you get older, some small bones join together to make big ones. By the time you graduate from high school, you will be down to 206 bones.

How do bones grow?

By layers. A thin layer of cartilage forms near the end of each bone. Cartilage is a tough, rubbery material that can bend. Gradually, the cartilage changes to bone, making the bone longer. As the bones get longer, they also get thicker. New layers of cartilage form throughout childhood and the teen years. When you are age 20 or so, all your cartilage layers will have turned to bone.

Do bones wear out?

Yes. The tiny cells of your bones are constantly dying and being replaced by new bone cells. In seven years, your body grows enough bone to make an entirely new skeleton!

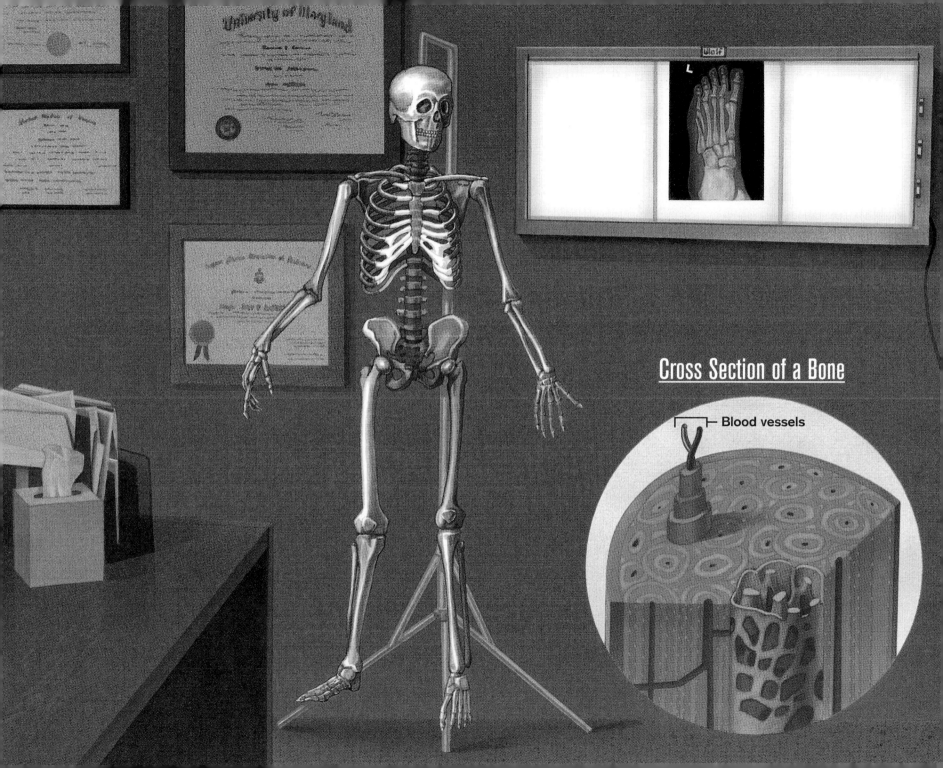

Cross Section of a Bone

Blood vessels

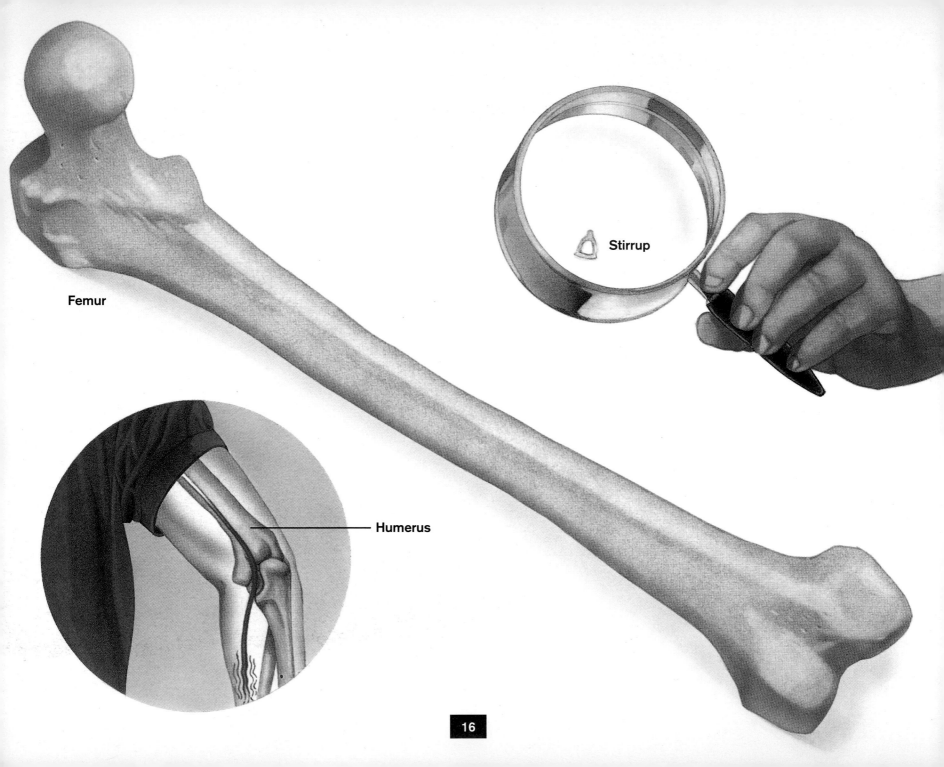

Femur

Humerus

Stirrup

Which are the biggest and smallest bones?

The thigh bone, or femur, is biggest. It is a strong, solid bone that can support your weight as you walk, run, dance, or kick. A femur can hold up a weight of more than one ton (1.016 t). Yet a blow from the side can break it quite easily.

The stapes, or stirrup, in your middle ear is the smallest bone in the body. It is just over 1/10 of an inch (.25 cm) long. The stirrup helps pass the vibrations of sound waves to your inner ear.

Which is the most useless bone in the body?

The coccyx. It is a small bone at the base of your spine. In a baby the coccyx is four little bones. They later join together to form one bone. But no one can figure out its purpose! Some say the coccyx is all that's left of a tail in ancestors that lived millions of years ago.

What is the "funny bone"?

A bone in your upper arm called the humerus. The word sounds like "humorous," or funny.

A nerve passes over the humerus at the elbow. If you hit your elbow, the nerve presses against the bone. This sends a tingling shock to your fingers that is far from funny!

Are bones the hardest things in the human body?

No. There is something that's even harder. It's the outside of your teeth. The enamel on your teeth is harder than your bones.

Why is your body able to bend?

Because it has joints. Joints are places where the bones of the skeleton fit together. Shoulders, elbows, and knees are all joints. So is the lower jaw that lets you open and close your mouth.

Your skeleton has more than 200 joints. Each hand has 40 or so in the wrist and fingers alone. Thanks to joints, you can tie your shoes, write with a pen, peel a banana—and do lots of other things.

Knee Joint

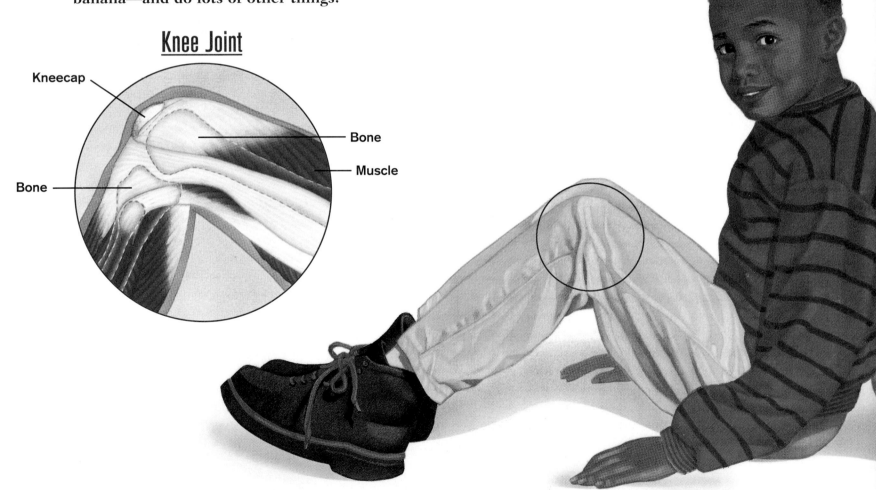

Kneecap

Bone

Bone

Muscle

What joins the bones to each other?

Strong bands of tissue called ligaments. When you bend a joint, the ligaments stretch and let the bones move. When you straighten up, the ligaments spring back like rubber bands.

Are you the same height all day long?

No. You're taller in the morning. During the day you get shorter. The pull of gravity squeezes the bones of your spine together. You can lose as much as 1 inch (2.5 cm) of height!

At night, when you're asleep in bed, the bones in your spine move slightly apart. In the morning, you're back to your full height.

Elbow Joint

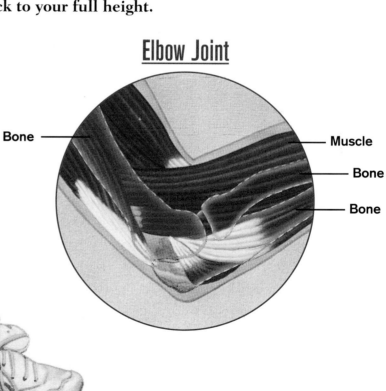

Bone — — Muscle

— Bone

— Bone

How do you move your bones?

Muscle power. Your muscles are like ropes. They pull on the bones to make them move. Altogether you have more than 600 muscles to move every part of your body.

Let's say you want to raise your forearm. You tighten muscles in your upper arm. They pull up your forearm. To lower your arm, you tighten other muscles. They pull your arm down.

What are muscles made of?

Long, strong fibers. Inside, a muscle looks something like the bunch of separate wires in a telephone cable.

Every muscle is teamed up with another muscle. You can feel a pair of muscles at work. Grab your right upper arm with your left hand. Now bend the right arm into a "strongman" pose. Feel how the top muscle, the biceps, bulges out. Next straighten your arm all the way. This time, you'll feel the triceps underneath grow bigger.

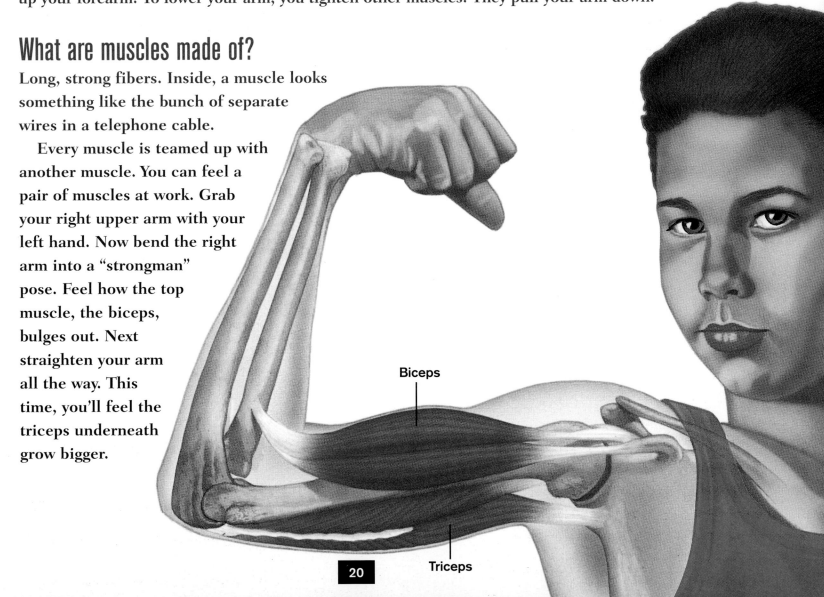

Biceps

Triceps

Why does the body need so many muscles?

To do everything from threading a needle to hitting a home run. Every movement uses dozens of muscles, big and small. Speaking takes 72 different muscles. To turn your foot you need 13 leg muscles and 20 foot muscles. Something as simple as taking a single step requires hundreds of muscles!

Which muscles get used the most?

The little muscles of the eye. They tighten and loosen about 100,000 times a day! You would have to walk about 50 miles (80 km) a day to give your legs that much exercise.

Which are the strongest muscles?

Not the biceps muscles in your arms! The strongest muscles, for their size, are the masseter muscles on the sides of your mouth. They let you bite with a force of 150 pounds (68 kg)!

Cross Section of a Muscle Fiber

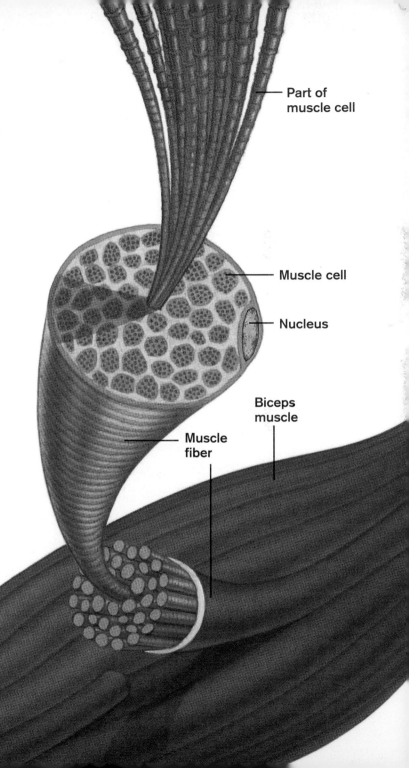

Part of muscle cell

Muscle cell

Nucleus

Biceps muscle

Muscle fiber

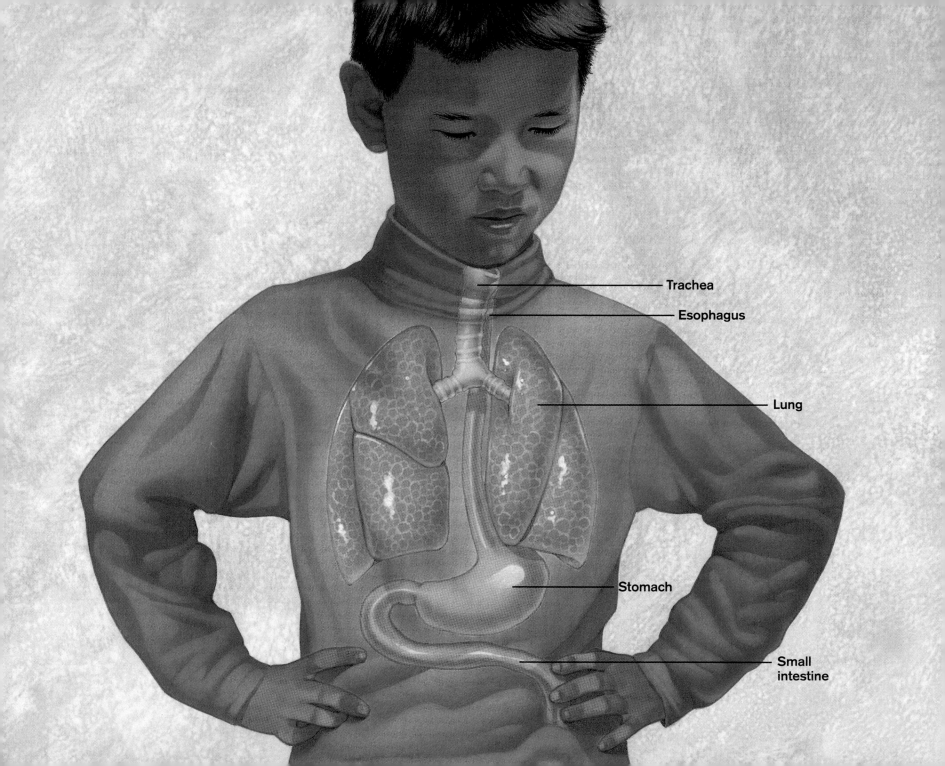

Trachea

Esophagus

Lung

Stomach

Small
intestine

Which muscles do you control?

The skeletal muscles. These are the muscles that are attached to your bones. You use them every time you walk or run, sit or stand, smile or frown.

Smooth muscles line your stomach, lungs, intestines, and other organs. You do not have to think about when and how to move these muscles.

What is your most movable organ?

Your tongue. It is made up of many small muscles that go in all different directions. And there are no bones to limit the ways it can move.

Is it easier to smile or to frown?

To smile. It takes about 17 muscles to create a smile. But it takes 43 muscles to make a frown. So smile—it's much easier—and friendlier.

What is a "charley horse"?

The sore feeling you get in muscles when you use them a lot. The term probably came from the use of "charley" to mean a horse that is lame.

To get rid of a charley horse, rest and massage the muscle. But don't take it too easy. Muscles must be used to stay strong. Regular exercise makes your muscles firmer and larger.

Why do you shiver?

To warm up. Shivering forces the muscles to tighten, relax, tighten, relax—over and over again, very fast. This gives off heat and raises the body's temperature.

How much food do you eat each year?

About half a ton (.5 t)! Your stomach and small intestine break the food down into tiny bits. These bits go into the body's cells to provide more energy and build more tissue.

How does your body turn pizza into energy?

By digestion. Chewing makes the pizza soft and starts the job of digestion. Strong muscles force the food through the food pipe, or esophagus, and into your stomach.

After a few hours in the stomach, the mushy pizza passes into the small intestine. Here different chemicals break the mush down into tiny specks. The bits pass through the walls of the small intestine and into the bloodstream.

The bloodstream carries the bits of food to cells all over the body. Each cell takes what it needs for energy and growth.

What causes stomach rumbles?

Food being digested. But the sound comes from your small intestine, not your stomach!

The small intestine pushes, squeezes, churns, and kneads the mashed-up food as it moves along. All this activity makes lots of noise. Just put your ear on someone's belly. You'll hear the terrific din of digestion.

If you eat at regular times each day, your stomach muscles will start to move on schedule. This causes stomach rumbles too. Your stomach may be telling you it's time to eat!

What makes a burp?

A bubble of gas from your stomach. The gas can be air that you swallowed while you ate, the fizzy bubbles from a glass of soda, or gas that formed as you digested your food. The rising gas makes your esophagus vibrate. This produces a sound. Excuse me! It's a burp.

Esophagus

Stomach

Large
intestine

Small
intestine

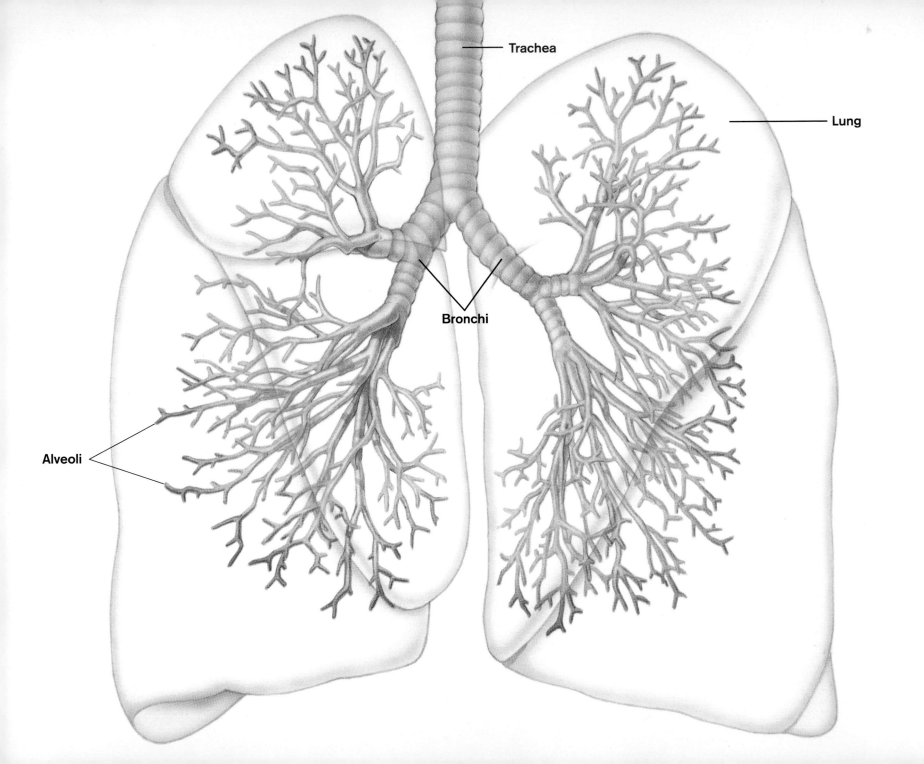

Why do you need to breathe?

To get oxygen. Oxygen is the gas in the air that your body needs to stay alive. The oxygen combines with other chemicals in your cells to produce energy. Every minute, your body needs about 8 quarts (7.6 l) of air if you're lying down, 24 quarts (22.8 l) of air if you're walking, and 50 or more quarts (47.5 l) if you're running.

The more active you are, the more energy you must produce. To make more energy, your body needs more oxygen. That's why you breathe faster when you are active.

What happens to air inside your lungs?

The air flows down your trachea, through the bronchi, into clusters of tiny balloonlike sacs called alveoli. The lungs have 300 million of these little air sacs. Altogether, they can hold as much air as a basketball.

Oxygen from the air passes into tiny blood vessels in the walls of the alveoli. Red blood cells in the bloodstream carry the oxygen to all your other cells. The cells use the oxygen to change food into energy.

What happens to the used-up oxygen?

It becomes a waste gas called carbon dioxide. The red blood cells in the blood pick up the carbon dioxide and bring it back to the lungs. The carbon dioxide passes into the alveoli. And, finally, you breathe out the carbon dioxide.

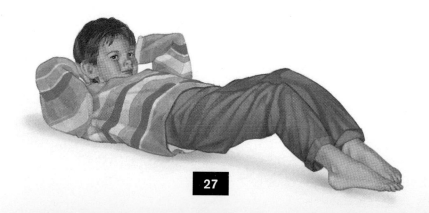

Why do you yawn?

No one knows for sure. Some people believe you yawn because you are not getting enough oxygen. Others say that yawning gets rid of extra carbon dioxide—which is why you feel so good after you yawn.

Any way you look at it, a really big yawn stretches your face and chest muscles. It improves the blood flow and wakes you up.

What are hiccups?

Little gasps of air. Hiccups start when a muscle at the bottom of the chest, called the diaphragm, suddenly tightens. It makes you take a quick breath. The rushing air slams shut the top of your windpipe, or trachea. This makes the vocal cords in the trachea produce the "hics" that give hiccups their name.

Who snores?

People who breathe through their mouth while asleep. The air sets the soft tissue at the back of the mouth into vibration. That produces the rough sound of snoring.

People with blocked noses often snore. Sometimes children with extra-large adenoids or tonsils snore as well. Usually, men snore more than women or children.

Why do you sneeze?

Because something tickles your nose. As you sneeze, air flies out of your mouth at over 100 miles (160 km) an hour! Mixed in with the air are thousands of germs that were in your nose. So remember—cover up when you sneeze!

You can sometimes stop a sneeze by pressing hard between your upper lip and nose. The nerve that brings the sneeze message to your nose passes there, and pressure can sometimes block the signal.

Heart

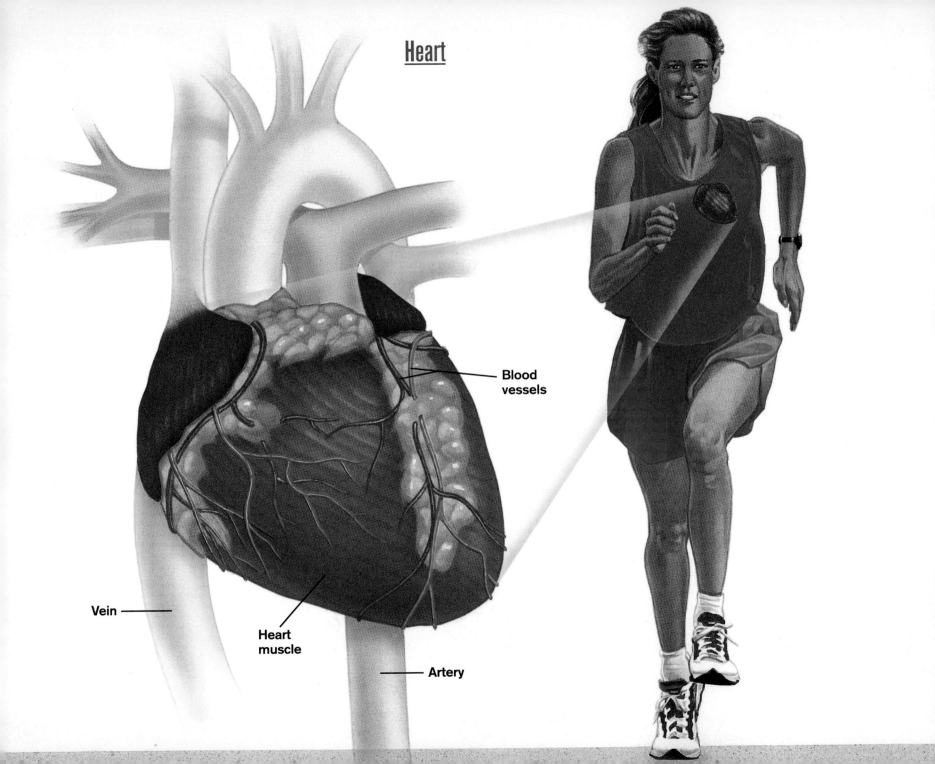

Blood vessels

Vein

Heart muscle

Artery

What makes your heart beat?

The muscles of the heart. The heart pumps blood throughout your body. It works day and night, whether you're asleep or awake.

Your heart started beating long before you were born. It sent blood through the few blood vessels that had already formed. During your lifetime it will beat nearly 3 billion times.

How big is your heart?

Not very big. No matter how old you are, your heart is just about the size of your clenched fist. And it is shaped more like your fist than like a valentine.

Where is your heart located?

Mostly in the middle of your chest. You may think the heart is on the left side. But that's because the bottom part of the heart leans that way. And that's the part that you can feel beating when you touch your chest.

What is your pulse?

The steady beat you can feel in your arteries. Each beat is a rush of blood pumped out by your heart.

Your pulse tells you how fast your heart is beating. To feel your pulse, lightly touch the skin on the inside of your wrist or your temple. Arteries are near the surface at these places.

Exercise and excitement make your heart speed up. The extra beats bring more oxygen-rich blood to the muscles. The heart also quickens when you get angry or frightened.

When you stop exercising or become calm, your heart slows down. It slows down most when you are asleep.

How fast does your heart beat?

It depends on your age. A baby's heart beats about 120 times a minute. The heart of a 10-year-old beats more slowly, about 90 times a minute. An adult heart is even slower, with just around 72 beats a minute.

The heart of an athlete is usually very well developed. Each beat pumps more blood. So an athlete's heart beats only 40 to 60 times a minute.

Can you hear your heartbeat?

No. What you hear are heart valves slapping closed. The heart has four parts, or chambers. The valves are flaps that open and close to let the blood flow from one chamber to another. The heartbeat itself is silent.

How do you measure blood pressure?

With an instrument called a sphygmomanometer (sfig-moh-muh-NOM-ih-tur). It measures the pressure of the blood flowing through your arteries. High blood pressure may be a sign of disease.

What is the difference between an artery and a vein?

An artery is a blood vessel that carries blood away from the heart to other parts of the body. A vein is a blood vessel that carries blood from around the body back toward the heart.

Very thin blood vessels link up the arteries and veins. They are called capillaries. Most capillaries are so narrow that the blood cells must pass through in single file!

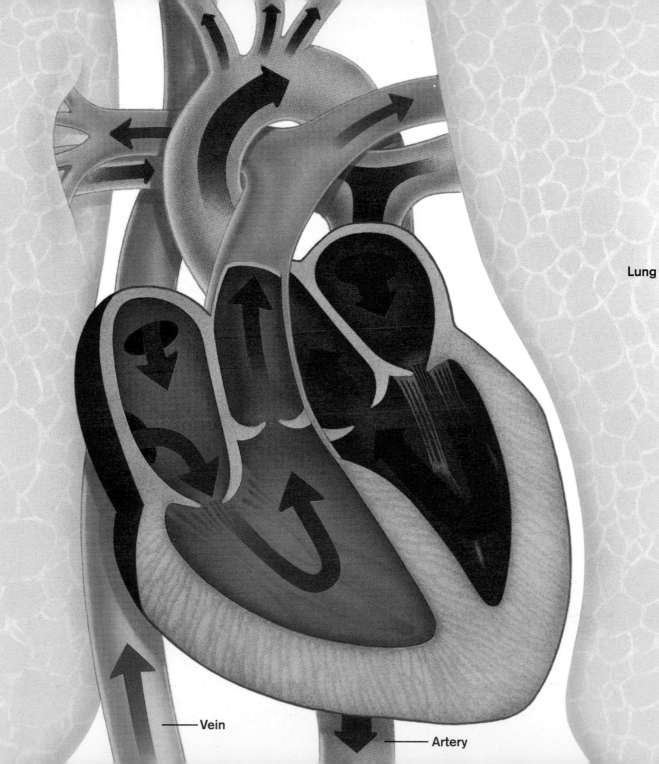

Cross Section
of the Heart

Lung

Lung

Vein

Artery

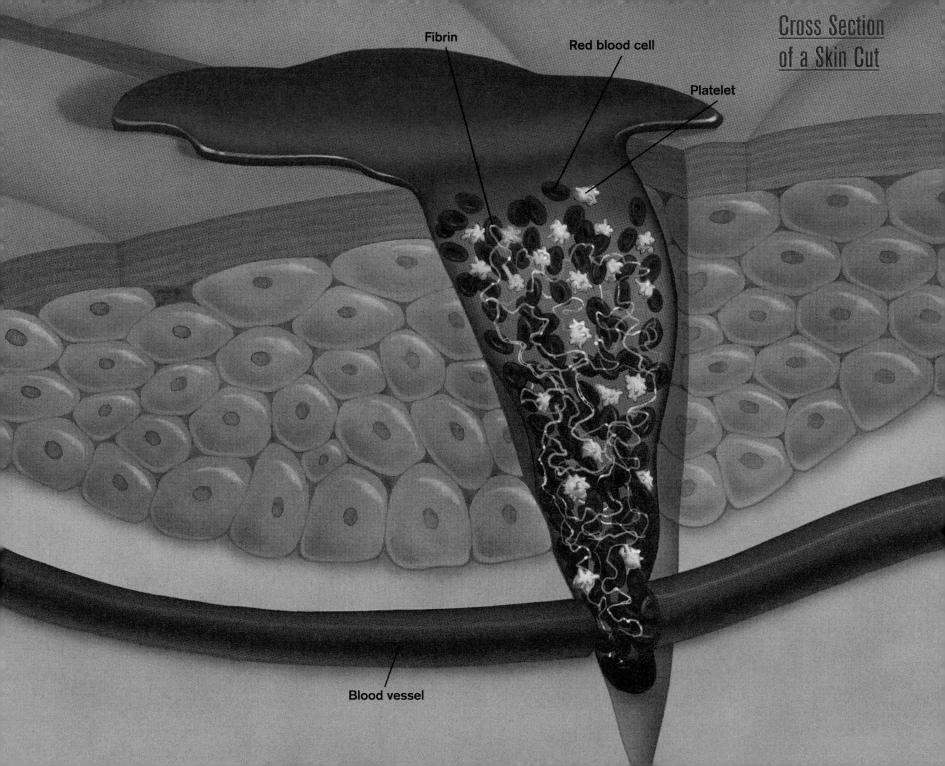

Fibrin

Red blood cell

Platelet

Blood vessel

What makes blood red?

The iron in red blood cells. The red blood cells carry oxygen from the lungs to all parts of your body. The body needs oxygen to stay alive.

The blood in arteries is bright red because the red blood cells are rich in oxygen. The blood in veins is purplish-red because the oxygen has passed out of the blood and into the cells of the body.

What makes a cut stop bleeding?

The blood itself. Chemicals in the blood form sticky threads called fibrin. The fibrin weaves a net that holds the red blood cells together. Tiny cell bits called platelets help form a plug, or clot. The clot stops the bleeding. Think of the clot as nature's bandage.

How much blood do you have?

About 3 quarts (2.8 l). Adults have about 5 quarts (4.7 l) of blood. The amount stays almost the same at all times.

Your blood flows through about 70,000 miles (112,000 km) of blood vessels. If you stretched them all out, they would wind almost three times around the equator!

Why do you blush?

Because tiny vessels in the skin suddenly expand and fill with blood. You blush when you feel nervous, embarrassed, or anxious, or have been very active. The extra blood makes your face and neck red and warm. If someone says, "You're blushing," you're sure to turn an even deeper red.

Which organ controls the whole body?

The brain. It is made up of millions of cells. Nerves from all over the body—except the organs of digestion—connect with the brain. Some go directly to the brain. Some go through the spinal cord.

The brain is always getting messages from inside the body. It also gets messages from the outside. They come through the sense organs—the eyes, ears, nose, tongue, and skin. And the brain is always sending messages out to every part of your body.

How fast does a signal travel through your nerves?

About 350 feet (10,500 cm) a second. Suppose you put your finger on a hot stove. The message speeds through nerve cells to your spinal cord and brain.

In a flash the brain sends a signal back through the nerves. "Leave!" the brain orders. Your muscles tighten and pull your finger away before you even know it.

Altogether, you have over 10 billion nerve cells. The network covers every part of your body.

Why does your leg "fall asleep"?

Usually because you are sitting too long in one position. Sometimes you get the "pins and needles" feeling because you are pressing on a nerve. Sometimes you get the same feeling because you are cramping a big blood vessel. Either way, your leg becomes numb or tingles.

There's only one thing to do. Move or walk around. Your leg will quickly "wake up," and you'll feel fine.

Why do you get pale when you are frightened?

Certain nerves make your blood vessels contract. This cuts the supply of blood to your face. As a result, you may look pale.

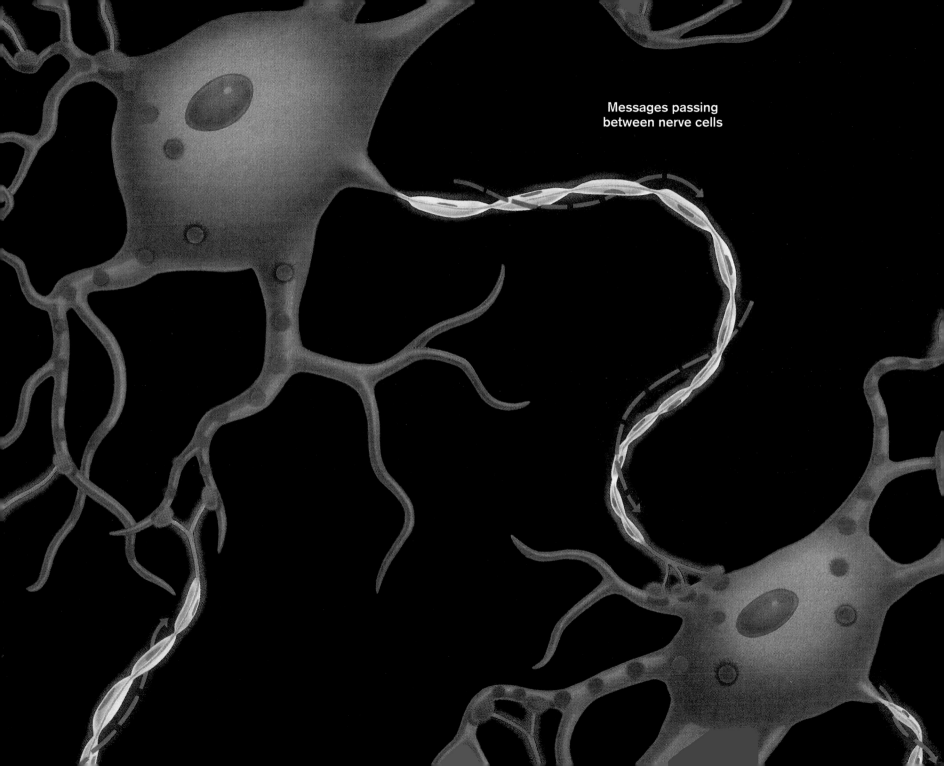

Messages passing
between nerve cells

How does human life begin?

As a single cell called a zygote. The zygote is made up of a sperm from a father and an egg from a mother. This single cell is the start of a new human being.

After a period of time, the cell splits and becomes two whole cells. Then each one splits again, and you have four cells, then 8, 16, 32, and so on. The cells keep on splitting and doubling in number. In time, the cells will number 26 *billion* for a child. And when the child grows up, he or she may have as many as 10 *trillion* cells!

What is the difference between fraternal twins and identical twins?

Fraternal twins develop from two separate zygotes. Each zygote is made up of one egg joined with one sperm. Fraternal twins are as alike as any brother and sister.

Identical twins develop from one zygote. But as the zygote divides, it forms two completely separate individuals. Identical twins look more alike than fraternal twins. About one out of every 90 births results in twins.

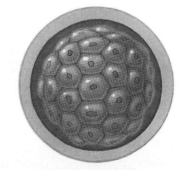
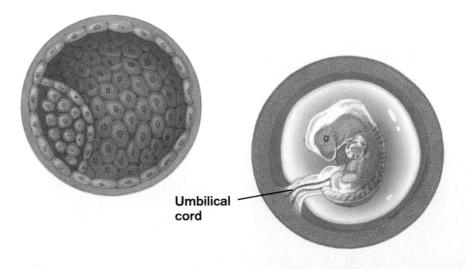

Umbilical
cord

What decides if the baby will be a boy or a girl?

Tiny threads called chromosomes. The chromosomes are found in the egg and sperm of the parents. At first, the mother's egg has two X chromosomes. The father's sperm has an X chromosome and a Y chromosome. When they are ready to join, the egg has one X and each sperm has either an X or a Y.

When a sperm with an X chromosome joins an egg, the zygote has two X chromosomes. The baby will be a girl. When a sperm with a Y chromosome joins an egg, the zygote has an X and a Y. That baby will be a boy.

When are most babies born?

In the early spring, on Tuesdays, between midnight and eight in the morning, and when there is a full moon. No one knows why, but that's what the figures show.

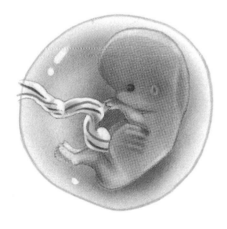

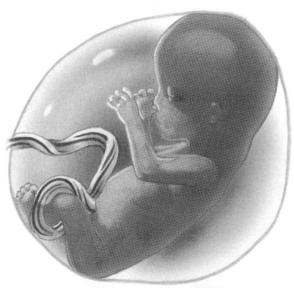

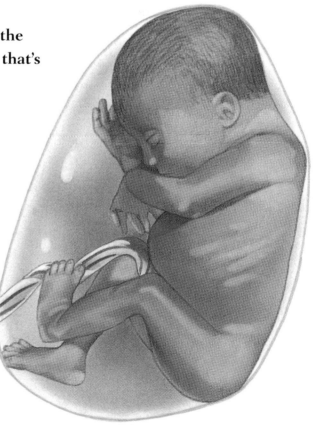

How does the unborn baby get food?

From the mother's body. The food passes through a long structure, called the umbilical cord, that contains blood vessels. It connects the mother to the unborn baby, or fetus. That's why the mother needs to eat lots of healthy food. The fetus also gets rid of waste through the umbilical cord.

After the baby is born, the doctor cuts the umbilical cord. You can touch the place where you were attached to your mother. It's your belly button!

By the time a baby is ready to be born, its umbilical cord is usually 2 feet (60 cm) long!

How long does the fetus stay in the mother's body?

Usually about nine months. Then the baby is ready to be born. At birth, the baby weighs about 7 pounds (3 kg) and is about 20 inches (50.8 cm) long.

The newborn can't walk or talk and has no teeth. The baby needs lots of love and care for a very long time. But within its body is everything it needs to become an adult man or woman.

Does a fetus have hair?

Yes. At 16 weeks the fetus has a light covering of hair on its head. As it develops, small amounts of soft, colorless hair grow all over its body. This hair is usually shed before birth.

Who had the most children of all?

Mrs. Feodor Vassilyev, of Russia. Between 1725 and 1765, she gave birth to 69 children: 16 pairs of twins, 7 sets of triplets, and 4 sets of quadruplets. And that was all before the days of disposable diapers!

A birth record was set on November 19, 1997, by Bobbi McCaughey in Des Moines, Iowa. She gave birth to seven babies—all born within minutes of one another.

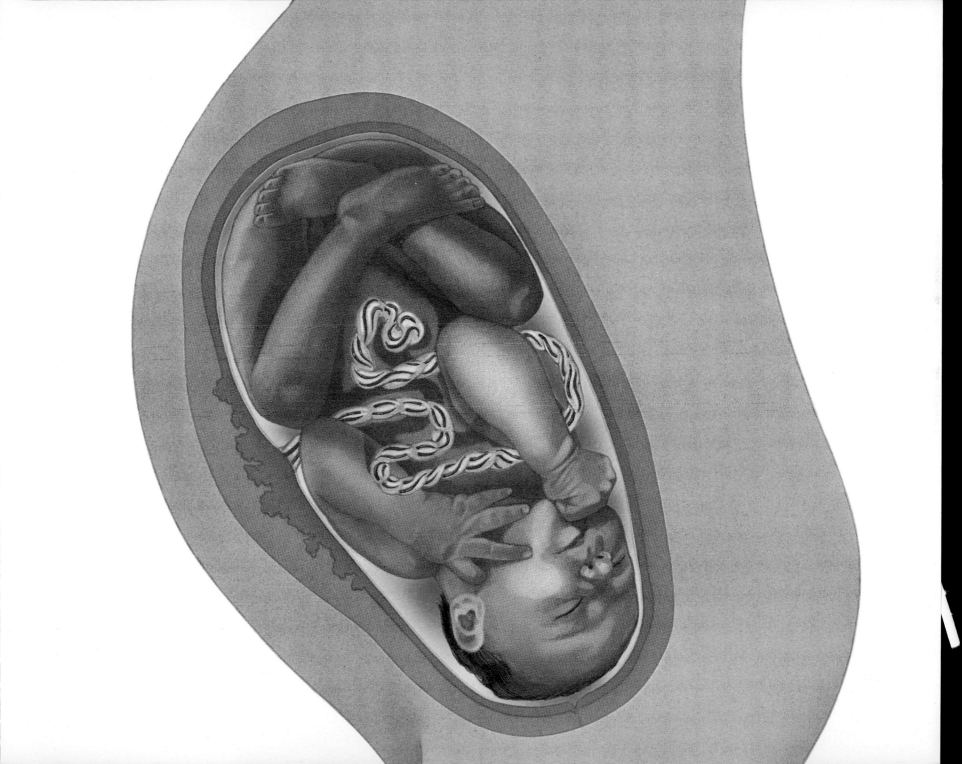

YOUR SENSES

How many senses do you have?

More than you think! First there are the five main senses: sight, hearing, smell, taste, and touch. But there are also many more: hunger, thirst, balance, fatigue, muscle tightness, and position of body parts.

Do you see with your eyes?

Not exactly. Your eyes pick up the light from objects, but it is your brain that actually "sees"!

Take the book you are reading. Light rays from the sun or from an electric light strike the book. The light bounces off and enters your eye. The rays pass through the eye and to the back of your eyeball, or retina.

In the retina, millions of tiny cells change the rays into electrical signals. The nerve signals flash to the brain. And your brain, not your eyes, figures out what you're seeing.

Why do you blink?

To keep your eyes clean and moist. If you're like most people, you blink once every six seconds. That means you blink more than 3 million times a year.

Each time you blink you keep your eyes shut for about one sixth of a second. At this rate your eyes are closed for nearly 200 hours every year from blinking alone!

What's the use of tears?

They wash the eyeballs and carry away dirt. Tears also contain salt and substances that kill germs.

All mammals produce tears to keep their eyes clean. Tears come from glands located under the eyelid of each eye. Two small tubes at the inner corner of each eyelid drain the tears from your eyes into your nose. That's why you almost always blow your nose after you have been crying.

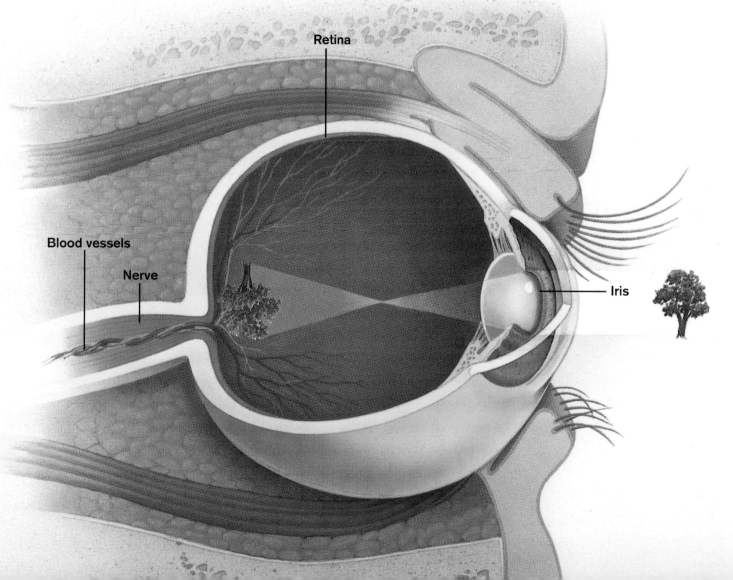

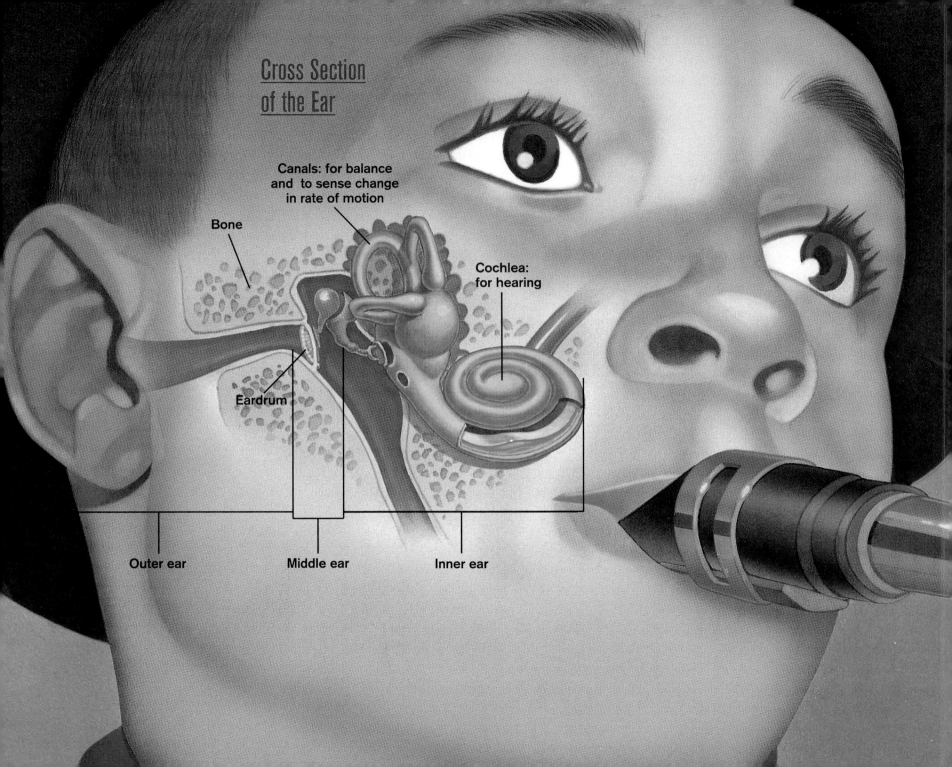

Cross Section
of the Ear

Canals: for balance
and to sense change
in rate of motion

Bone

Cochlea:
for hearing

Eardrum

Outer ear

Middle ear

Inner ear

How do you hear?

Your ears pick up sound waves in the air. For example, a dog barks. The bark makes the air vibrate, forming invisible sound waves. The waves pass through the three parts of your ear—the outer ear, the middle ear, and the inner ear. Nerve endings in the inner ear send electrical signals to your brain. And you hear the sound.

Why do you need two ears?

To tell the direction of a sound. For example, a fire truck clangs its bell. The sound enters your right ear a tiny bit sooner than it enters your left ear. Also the sound is a tiny bit louder in the right ear. Your brain notes the slight difference in time and loudness. It lets you know that the sound is coming from the right. It also lets you know how far away it is.

Can loud noises make you lose your hearing?

Yes. Loud noises can damage the eardrum or harm the cells in your inner ear.

A single loud noise, like a fire siren, can affect your hearing for a short time. But repeated loud sounds, like highly amplified music, can cause permanent damage. The result can be a loss of hearing.

What makes you dizzy after you spin around?

The fluid in your inner ear. After you spin around, the fluid keeps on spinning. This sends mixed-up signals to the brain. You lose your sense of balance. You feel dizzy. You may even topple over.

In a few moments, the liquid levels out. The dizzy feeling goes away.

How many odors can you smell?

About 10,000 different ones, on average. But that's not as good as it gets. Some perfume experts can recognize about 30,000 separate scents!

How do you pick up smells?

With your nose. Let's say someone is baking cookies. The smell comes into your nose with the air. It strikes a spot in the back, top part of your nose. Here thousands of tiny cells pick up the cookie smell. They send a message to your brain. Right away, your brain knows that cookies are baking.

How do you get the taste of food?

From taste buds. You have 9,000 tiny bumps on your tongue. Every bump has about 250 taste buds. The taste buds can pick up four basic flavors—sweet, salty, sour, and bitter. You have extra taste buds around your mouth. Altogether, they give you the taste of your food.

Taste buds need the help of your nose. Unless you can smell the food, you can't taste it. So if your nose is stuffed, it's hard to tell an apple from an onion!

What is the most important sense?

Some experts think sight. Others say hearing. The fact is, no one sense is *most* important. It takes all of your senses, as sharp and alert as possible, to experience the wonderful world around you.

The senses are one of the systems in your body. Keep all of them working well and you'll enjoy being the unique and special person that you are.

Index

About the Authors

The Bergers have long wondered why haircuts don't hurt. "We wrote this book to share what we learned about hair—and about other parts of ourselves. The research renewed our appreciation for the remarkable human body."

About the Illustrator

Karen Barnes knew she loved to draw when she was in kindergarten. In school she won many awards and even won money for college. Karen lives in Maryland with her husband, John, and two rambunctious cats.